# IS IT TRUE THAT RESTITUTION OF MARITAL RIGHTS INFRINGES ON ONE'S RIGHT TO PRIVACY?

VOLUME 2, ISSUE 1 OF BRILLOPEDIA

SHWETA VINOD YADAV

ISBN 979-888606517-6

# Contents

*Preface* *v*

*Publication* *vii*

*Author* *ix*

1. Abstract 1
2. Introduction 2
3. The Procedure To Be Undertaken In Order To Reclaim Conjugal Rights 4
4. Restitution Of Conjugal Right's Consitutionality 5
5. Why Should It Be Removed In The First Place? 8
6. Conclusion 10

# Preface

"Start writing, no matter what. The water does not flow until the faucet is turned on".

-Louis L'Amour

Hundreds of students and professors are contributing their work to Brillopedia, we are here to provide ample information about Law and Contemporary issues. Our aim is to provide a platform for today's generation to express their views and ideas on law and contemporary law.

# Publication

This research paper is published in volume 2, issue 1 of Brillopedia

# Author

Shweta Vinod Yadav

CHAPTER ONE

# ABSTRACT

Essentially conjugal rights are rights conferred by marriage, such as the right of a husband or wife to the other spouse's society. These rights are recognised by the law, both in personal law (marriage, divorce, etc.) and in criminal law (maintenance and alimony payments to a spouse). Section 9 of the Hindu Marriage Act recognises and protects one facet of conjugal rights: the right to consortium, by permitting a spouse to file a court action to enforce the right. Restitution of conjugal rights is presently established in Hindu personal law, but it has colonial roots and its foundations in ecclesiastical law. Similar restrictions can be found in Muslim personal law as well as the Christian Divorce Act of 1869. The statute on restitution of marital rights was repealed in the United Kingdom in 1970. This article examines the right to privacy as well as the issue of restitution in the context of privacy law. The purpose of this article is to critically examine the notion of Restitution of Conjugal Rights, a matrimonial remedy provided for Hindus under the Hindu Marriage Act of 1955. In addition the restitution of conjugal rights remedy is a positive remedy that requires both spouses to live together and cohabit. This cure, however, has been abused. As a result, questions have been raised as to whether this is, in fact, a cure.

**Keywords**: Restitution of conjugal rights, Privacy, Marriage, Constitution

CHAPTER TWO

# INTRODUCTION

Marriage is a sacred relationship that ensures the coexistence of opposing viewpoints. For the sake of convenience, each wife has the right to the other's consortium. It is a lifelong commitment between the parties to live in harmony for the rest of their lives. Each side is entitled to certain benefits from the other. As a result, several laws have been codified, such as the Hindu Marriage Act of 1955, to ensure that these rights are universal. As a result, it is a treatment.

Following their solemnization of marriage, both husband and wife are legally committed to keep their marital life together and are entitled to the enjoyment of rights and the obligation of duties. If either spouse separates from the other, the aggrieved spouse may be able to get a matrimonial remedy guarantee under personal laws, allowing him or her to restore his or her status to the other person subject to verification of specific conditions. This can be accomplished by filing a re-establishment of coexistence petition with the tribunal. Conjugal Rights is the name given to this type of privilege. These are referred to as "common law" rights. The term 'conjugal' signifies 'wedlock' in theory.

If either spouse or spouse has withdrew from society without good reason, the aggrieved group may request a refund of marriage privileges through a petition to the district court, and the court, if satisfied by the truth of the statements made in the petition and there is no lawful reason why the request should not be granted, may restore the order.Because there is no legal relationship, the request for restitution of marital rights cannot be sustained, It is the responsibility of the person who has retreated from society to present a good explanation for doing so.

**ESSENTIALS**

- Withdrawal from the social group.

- There must be no justification, excuse, or legitimate basis for the withdrawal.
- There should be no other legal basis for rejecting relief.
- The truth of the statement provided in the petition must satisfy the court.

It's a strategy for avoiding divorce in marriage, and it's a good one because it necessitates the cohabitation of both spouses.

CHAPTER THREE

# THE PROCEDURE TO BE UNDERTAKEN IN ORDER TO RECLAIM CONJUGAL RIGHTS

- The reparation suit petition is filed in district court by the aggrieved spouse. The petitioner then sends the case application to the HC
- The reparation suit petition is filed in district court by the aggrieved spouse. The petitioner then sends the case application to the HC.
- On the appointed days, both parties should appear in court.
- After that, the court will send both parties to counselling sessions. Typically, these courts hold three sessions over the course of four months, with a 20-day gap between them.
- Finally, the judge will issue a decree based on the parties' descriptions and the counselling sessions.

CHAPTER FOUR

# RESTITUTION OF CONJUGAL RIGHT'S CONSITUTIONALITY

The constitutional validity of Section 9 was first contested in *T Sareeta v Venkatasubbiah*, in which the Andhra Pradesh High Court found Section 9 of the Hindu Marriage Act to be invalid and declared it to be a violation of the Constitution.

Section 9 was declared unlawful by Justice Chaudhary because it was a "savage and brutal remedy" that violated the right to privacy and human dignity provided by Article 21 of the Constitution.In delivering the verdict, Justice Chaudhary analysed the history and effectiveness of the remedy, concluding that "Section 9 promotes no justifiable goal based on any idea of the general welfare. It does not contribute to any societal good.

When Justice Chaudhary's dicta was challenged in *Harvinder Kaur v Harminder Singh*,the Delhi High Court did not agree. "Justice Chaudhary in the matter of T. Sareetha has over-relied on sex is the primary mistake in his conclusion," Justice Rohtagi said. According to J. Rohtagi, J. Chaudhary merely seems to imply that the restitution of conjugal rights order serves just a secondary aim, namely, forcing the disinclined wife to engage in sexual intercourse with her husband.

Finally, in *Saroj Rani v Sudarshan Kumar Chadha*,the Supreme Court reversed T Sareeta, relying on Justice Rotagi's decision in Harvinder Kaur. "It cannot be viewed in the manner in which the learned single Judge bench of the Andhra Pradesh High Court has viewed it," Justice Sabyasachi Mukarji said, "and we are unable to hold that Section 9 is violative of Article 14 and Article 21 of the Constitution." In the legal sphere, the apex court ruled in favour of Section 9 of the Hindu Marriage Act of 1955, and the most importantly the notion of restitution of conjugal rights is constitutional in the Indian legal system.

The Court stated that the remedy's sole goal is cohabitation, not compelling sexual intercourse between the unwilling couple, as required by Article 21 of the Constitution. The integration of Constitutional Law into family law has been condemned by the court as a brutal destroyer of the institution of marriage.

The Restitution Decree's sole purpose was to promote a united marriage and prevent a reluctant lady from having sexual relations with her husband. The sole goal was to achieve 'cohabitation' between spouses, hence the term 'consortium' was used sparingly.

The Supreme Court and the Delhi High Court, on the other hand, may not have recognised that marital rape was allowed in India. Except in the case of a long-drawn-out petition for divorce based on cruelty or a petition for domestic abuse based on sexual violence, the husband can compel his wife into sexual relationships with no consequences. In fact, by submitting an unwilled wife to "forced cohabitation" and "consortium," the decree effectively puts a wife under the pressure of forceful sex with her husband while also stripping her of physical autonomy, dignity, and the basic freedom to make her own choices relating to her own life and body.

1. **The Constitution's Article 14**

While both husband and wife can seek restitution of conjugal rights, the fundamental inequalities between men and women cannot be overlooked when assessing the remedy from a socio-legal standpoint. Although a remedy is not readily available in society, we should not neglect the reality that most women still have a lower social and financial status in society than men.

The right to equality and the right to life are both violated when marital rights are restored. Equality entails the same level of thought, behaviour, and self-awareness. The continuing of the cure leads to unwanted pregnancies, according to the argument, and it violates women's feelings of respect, dignity, and personal fulfilment.

By mandating who a person must live with, the remedy for the Restitution of Conjugal Rights undermines the basic nature of a person. In our largely patriarchal countries, both married couples are not necessarily equal, and the wife is mostly socially and economically dependent on the husband.Because of illiteracy, economic reliance, and other causes, males in a man-dominated society frequently reap the benefits of many laws and remedies. Because the woman is usually placed in an adverse situation, there is only one clear trait.

## 1. Article 21 of the Constitution (Right to Privacy)

The right to privacy (Article 21 of the Constitution) is not explicitly protected by the law. There is no universally accepted definition of privacy.The Supreme Court's first case on the right to privacy was *Kharak Singh v State of Uttar Pradesh.*Any concept of privacy must cover and safeguard the personal intimacies of the home, family, marriage, maternity, procreation, and child-rearing, Justice Subba Rao stated.

The Court established that the right to privacy is a basic right in *Govind v State of MP*, but it was contained in the liberty clause like its American counterpart. "Any right to privacy must encircle and preserve the intimate intimacies of the home, the family, marriage, motherhood, procreation, and child-rearing" Justice Mathew said.

Setting individual limitations and limiting the admission of others into this area is a natural necessity for a person. As a right, privacy is difficult to define because its contours are yet unknown. It is not a unity concept, but it is more susceptible to enumeration than a multi-dimensional definition.

CHAPTER FIVE

# WHY SHOULD IT BE REMOVED IN THE FIRST PLACE?

The main goal of restoring conjugal rights is for husband and wife to reconcile so that their marriage might be saved. Individuals, on the other hand, often have different goals in mind when applying for the same. Furthermore, section 13 (1-A) of the Hindu Marriage Act, 1955 states that if it is not observed, it can be used as grounds for divorce. This contradicts Section 9's stated purpose of avoiding divorce.

If an individual fails to comply with the decree, the Court has the authority to enforce it. According to Rule 32, the Court may attach the decree holder's property by selling it within six months. When the woman, on the other hand, does not own any property, as is the case in India. This is a concern because her share of her husband's estate is calculated using a formula.

**WHY SHOULD IT BE KEPT IN PLACE?**

Simply because a part has the potential to be misinterpreted does not mean it should be eliminated. Its goal is to restore cohabitation and save one of the most important aspects of marriage. If nothing is wrong with the marriage or the way agreement was obtained there is no reason to prohibit cohabitation.As well as right to conjugal union is restored. And If one of the spouses withdraws from the other's company without good reason, the other aggrieved party has the legal right to file a petition for the restitution of conjugal rights. The court can issue such a decision if it is satisfied that the petition is true and that there is no legal reason to prevent them from doing so. However burden of proof is on the person who has withdrawn from society if they have a reasonable cause for doing so.

Nevertheless If restitution is not paid within a year, it may be grounds for divorce. However, the argument given for this is that a marriage should not be broken up suddenly. The one-year time is necessary as a "cooling phase" to avoid making a hasty decision. Even if there is no cohabitation, it allows for divorce. It ensures that divorce is granted only after all other options for reviving the marriage have been exhausted.

CHAPTER SIX

# CONCLUSION

A restitution of conjugal rights decree can require spouses to live together but it can't guarantee a healthy relationship. Furthermore, if the decree infringes on any constitutional right, it is critical that it be repealed. With all of the ambiguities that exist within the sections pertaining to restitution of conjugal rights.It is imperative that the Supreme Court investigate the matter and ensure that this right, which is considered a remedy does not violate anyone's fundamental rights and that if it does, it is declared unconstitutional as soon as possible.

Restitution of marital rights is governed by the individual's own rules which are guided by principles such as religion, tradition, and custom. The fact that restitution of conjugal rights is a remedy targeted at preserving the marriage rather than disturbing it, as is the case with divorce or legal separation, is an important characteristic to emphasise. It aids in the avoidance of marriage dissolution and thus acts as a means of saving the marriage. If a decree of restitution of conjugal rights or the right to remain together is not followed for more than one year after the date of the decree, it can be used as a basis for divorce.

As a result, the restitution of conjugal rights remedy aims to promote reconciliation between the parties and the preservation of the married relationship. It strives to keep society from being degraded. Howeverthe parties must make the final decision whether to obey the ruling of restitution of conjugal rights and continue the matrimony or not.

www.ingramcontent.com/pod-product-compliance
Ingram Content Group UK Ltd.
Pitfield, Milton Keynes, MK11 3LW, UK
UKHW021926190726
13853UKWH00002B/869

9 798886 065176